GREY

Koko Brown

GREY

OBERON BOOKS
LONDON

WWW.OBERONBOOKS.COM

First published in 2019 by Oberon Books Ltd
521 Caledonian Road, London N7 9RH
Tel: +44 (0.) 20 7607 3637 / Fax: +44 (0.) 20 7607 3629
e-mail: info@oberonbooks.com
www.oberonbooks.com

PB ISBN: 9781786827944
E ISBN: 9781786827951

Cover photography: Susan Dale
Cover design: Chris Lincé

Printed and bound by 4EDGE Limited, Hockley, Essex, UK.
eBook conversion by Lapiz Digital Services, India.

Visit www.oberonbooks.com to read more about all our books and to buy them. You will
also find features, author interviews and news of any author events, and you can sign up for
e-newsletters so that you're always first to hear about our new releases.

Printed on FSC® accredited paper

10 9 8 7 6 5 4 3 2 1

An early version of the play was first performed at Ovalhouse Theatre, London, on 27th September 2018. The updated version premiered at Ovalhouse Theatre, London, on 27th June 2019.

CHARACTERS

Woman	Koko Brown
Her	Sapphire Joy

CREATIVE TEAM

Director	Nicholai La Barrie
Set & Costume Designer	Emily Harwood
Lighting Designer	Martha Godfrey
Movement Director	Shelley Maxwell
Sound Designer	Xana

*

The characters are age non-specific. This play incorporates music, and performers are encouraged to use an instrument and/or style that suits them. The performer is encouraged to find their own rhythm within the poetry.

WOMAN primarily speaks in English and sometimes signs in British Sign Language (BSL). HER only signs in BSL. It is assumed that they interpret for each other, unless otherwise stated.

There is pre-show music playing while the audience enter. The song choice should be made up of Black female musicians that the cast would have listened to.

For the Black women that stood before me,
that walk with me
and will thrive after me

For Abeo, Akilah and Chantelle

For anyone who has ever felt like *the other*

PROLOGUE

WOMAN enters.

So there's a girl. She's standing on a cliff. She looks out.
In the distance she sees a sea of tall, green trees. She sees
still, serene mountains. She sees a vast, blue sky.

She feels the breeze on her face and, as she walks towards
the edge of the cliff, she inhales deeply.

As she steps forward, she feels the ground shift. She looks
back and sees a crack has formed.

A small but sinister crack has formed.

She knows what comes next. She has to make a choice.
She has to make a decision.

She has to decide whether to go back, leap over the
crack, return to land that seems so stable, or throw herself
forward, off the edge, and hope she lands on something
soft, or stay exactly where she is, unmoving, and hope that
the ground doesn't fall from under her.

HELLA SAD

HER enters.

A descending, rhythmic melody begins. It is layered with clicks, bass-like synth sounds, low rhythms and high adlibs.

> I'VE TRIED RUNNING AND FIGHTING
> AND LAUGHING AND FIGHTING
> AND LYING AND FIGHTING
> AND CRYING AND FIGHTING
>
> I'VE TRIED CBT
> I'VE TRIED UNLOCKING THINGS
> TALKING ABOUT THE TRAUMA
> ALL THE CHILDHOOD TRAUMA
>
> I'VE TRIED EVERYTHING UNDER THE SUN
> I'VE TRIED MEDITATION
> I'VE TRIED YOGA,
> OVER AND OVER
>
> BUT NOTHING SEEMS TO WORK
> NO, NOTHING SEEMS TO WORK
> SO I SIT AND DROWN IN ALL OF THIS HURT
>
> I AM HELLA SAD,
> I AM HELLA SAD
> I'M REALLY REALLY REALLY REALLY REALLY
> REALLY SAD
> ALL OF THE TIME, ALL OF THE TIME (ALL OF
> THE TIME)

What do you mean you're not sad all of the time?
What do you mean you don't want to cry all of the time?
What do you mean it's a chemical imbalance in my mind?

No, no, no no I'm fine. I'm fine.
Yeah I'm sure, I'm fine.
I'm just tired.
It's just because I'm tired.
I'm tired of feeling so tired, ya know?

I'm just a little overworked.
Yeah I've been drinking water.
Yeah I've been taking breaks.
Yeah I'm sure, I'm sure, I'm sure I've eaten today.

I should have a hot bath? … Yeah I'll totally try that.
I should do a face mask? … Yeah I'll totally try that.
I should listen to whale sounds? … Yeah I'll totally try that.
I should write my feelings down? … Yeah I'll totally try that.

Sorry I've got to cancel.
                    I know that we booked a table.
I know that it's my birthday.
                    I know it's been planned for ages.
I know people are expecting me.
I know they were looking forward to this. I know they'll
be disappointed.
But they'll get over it.

I'm just a little under the weather.
Yeah, the flu or something.
Yeah, stomach bug or something.
Yeah, migraine or something.
No, no, don't worry, it's nothing.

No, it's nothing.

Nothing's happened to me.

Yeah I'm fine, really.

Yeah I'm sure, yeah… *(Ad-libbing.)*

It's just weird because–

> I'M REALLY SAD, LIKE, ALL OF THE TIME,
> BUT I SMILE SMILE SMILE SMILE ALL OF THE TIME
>
> I FEEL REALLY UNHAPPY
> LIKE ALL THE TIME UNHAPPY
> HAPPY, HAPPY, HAPPY, HAPPY
> WHY CAN'T I JUST BE HAPPY?
>
> I FEEL LIKE I'M DYING
> I WISH I WAS DYING
> *(Repeats.)*
>
> WOAH
> I WISH THAT I WAS DYING
> WOAH
> I WISH THAT I WAS DYING
> WOAH

Music fades out.

'Cause then I'd have a reason to feel this sad.

CLUBHOUSE

A finger click is brought in. WOMAN then brings in the Clubhouse melody. It is fun and playful like a children's television show theme.

> OOH OOH OOH,
> OOH OOH OOH,
> OOH OOH OOH,
> OOH! OOH! OOH!
> *(Repeats.)*
>
> WELCOME TO THE CLUBHOUSE
> WELCOME TO THE CLUBHOUSE
> WELCOME TO THE CLUBHOUSE
> COME ON IN!
> *(Repeats.)*
>
> *(Riffing.)*
> WELCOME TO THE CLUBHOUSE
> WELCOME TO THE CLUBHOUSE
> WELCOME TO THE CLUBHOUSE
> COME ON IN!

HER stops the music.

WOMAN: Hey there! Welcome to The Clubhouse, it's nice to see you!

HER: Today we're going to meet our new friend Sadness. Where's Sadness?

WOMAN: Where is Sadness? Shall we call her?

BOTH: Sadness! Sadness! Sadness!

WOMAN creates a puppet with her hand.

WOMAN: Here she is!

HER: Can we spell Sadness? S-A-D-N-E-S-S.

BOTH: Great job!

HER: Sadness is an emotion. Emotions are those little things inside of us which tell us how we feel.

WOMAN: Sometimes I feel happy! When I feel happy I make this face. Sometimes I like to play with my friends and go out to dance in clubs with sticky floors! Have you ever been happy?

HER: Sometimes I feel angry! When I'm angry I make this face. Sometimes I slam doors and tell people to 'go fuck themselves'. Have you ever been angry?

WOMAN: Sometimes I feel sad. When I'm sad I make this face. Sometimes I am very quiet and I cry for hours on end. Have you ever been sad?

HER: If you are very sad for a very long time, some people call this depression. Can we spell 'depression'? D-E-P-R-E-S-S-I-O-N.

BOTH: Great job!

WOMAN: According to the smart people at some survey company, 350 million people suffer from depression. Only one third will get help.

HER: Aren't we talking about Black people?

WOMAN: Yes! We are talking about Black people! So let me start that again…

According to the smart people at some survey company, 350 million people suffer from depression. Only one third will get help. If you're a Black person, you have the same chance of suffering from depression, or another mental illness, but significantly less of those will seek help.

HER: But doesn't that mean that Black people are more likely to suffer from undiagnosed mental illnesses for a longer amount of time and potentially increase their risk of worsening their illness or committing suicide?

WOMAN: Wow you're really knowledgeable! And, yes, it does mean all of those things and more!

HER: Wow, that sounds exhausting and really detrimental to the Black community!

WOMAN: It is!

They laugh.

HER: Thank you for visiting us today, Sadness. I think it's time to say goodbye!

BOTH: Goodbye!

Sadness stays.

Goodbye!

Sadness stays.

Goodbye!

Sadness leaves.

WOMAN: *(To HER.)* Goodbye sadness. Goodbye.

DEPRESSION IS...

WOMAN begins to loop low melodies on top of one another. This is done with pace and urgency.

> HOW AM I SUPPOSED TO FEED A MIND,
> INSIDE A BODY, THAT'S TRYING TO KILL ME?
> HOW AM I SUPPOSED TO LIVE A LIFE,
> INSIDE THIS BODY, WITH A MIND THAT'S
> TRYING TO KILL ME?

WOMAN: You see, depression isn't pretty. It's not poetic.
It's ugly.

It's sitting on the toilet, taking a piss, and suddenly, out of
nowhere, bursting into tears. Crying your eyes out.

Crying. And peeing. And peeing. And crying. And not
being able to stop crying while you're peeing.

So you sit and pee and cry. And you don't move until
you've stopped peeing or crying.

It's when you're having an episode that's so bad.

You think that, instead of going for a walk or calling a friend
or trying any of that other really useful self-care stuff that
your therapist tells you about, you think that it's safer to stay
exactly where you are, because if you stay exactly where
you are, then there is nothing to hurt you. Except you.

And because your mind knows this it flips through the
Rolodex of all the shitty things that you've done and all

the bad things that have happened to you and mixes them in with a list of reasons that you deserve it.

So you sit there and let it happen because you're spiralling down so fast that the only thing that you can control is whether you physically move or not.

And you put so much energy into not moving, that you tense all your muscles. And you start shaking. Or, you wonder, were you shaking before you were tensing? You don't really know.

You just know that you're tensing so hard and shaking so much and crying so uncontrollably that you've given yourself a migraine.

It's wanting to bail on going out with your friends because you feel so volatile, so unhinged, that you just know tonight is the night that you're gonna go out, try and drink through it all and end up getting in a fight with a stranger over something stupid. Like them dancing too close to you. Or them being served first at the bar. And you know it's going to ruin what was already a hopeless night.

So, you'll leave before everyone else.

And while standing on the platform waiting for the train, you wonder if you should just throw yourself under the next one, but then decide against it because that's the last train of the night and if you throw yourself in front of this one, then it would put it out of service and the people who thought they could catch the last train to get home actually now have to get a night bus which would be really inconvenient for them.

And so you don't do it.

Instead you get on, you sit down and focus all your energy on not crying because the train's bright and it will be obvious that you're crying and some kind, slightly drunk person will ask you what the matter is and you don't know how you'll be able to answer that because you don't know what's the matter. You're just sad.

So you stay quiet, fight the tears and just wait it out until you get home.

WOMAN begins interpreting with HER.

Sometimes it's nothing like any of that.

But it's never beautiful. It is not poetic words about being in a dark place. Sometimes it's nothing.

It's feeling nothing. You don't feel happy. But you don't feel sad either. You're just void of feeling. You don't want to cry or scream or talk or anything. You just feel real numb. Empty.

And that's the worst because, at that time, in that moment, you're not even whole enough to feel anything. You're so broken that instead, you're just the gaps between the fragments of the person that you were.

HOW AM I SUPPOSED TO LIVE A LIFE, INSIDE THIS BODY, WITH A MIND THAT'S TRYING TO KILL ME?

I ALWAYS KNEW WHAT I WAS

WOMAN begins to loop bouncy, doo-wop style music that underscores the scene. Layers are added and removed throughout to add emphasis where it feels appropriate.

WOMAN: I always knew what I was.

> I was female. I was Black. Aged 1.
> I was happy.
> Anything would make me happy. Everything made me happy.
> The colour green made me happy. Grapes made me happy.
> The fact that grapes were green made me happy.
> Because what have you got to be sad about when you're 1?

> I always knew what I was.
> I was female. I was Black. Aged 13.
> I was ashamed.
> Felt shame 'cause the boy I liked, about this tall, spiky hair, fair, always wore Nike Air
> Max was his name, said I was the last person he'd ever wanna date.
> I was crushed but I got over it because, what have you really got to be sad about when you're 13?

> I always knew what I was.
> I was female. I was Black.
> Aged 6. I was miserable.
> Something was stirring at school and so Sharna and Charlotte split, saying
> 'We're not your friends anymore.'

I always knew what I was.
I was female. I was Black. Aged 18.
I was proud.
Proud I'd made it through my 18th birthday without
throwing up…in public.

I always knew what I was.
I was female. I was Black. Aged 22.
New year, new you.
The new you, knew you were still in there somewhere,
Hiding behind the shambolically simulated smile.

I always knew what I was.
I was female. I was Black. Aged 19.
Nightly cram sessions ensured I excelled.
Passed with ease. Sigh of relief. And I was free.
Free to be whoever I wanted to be.
Fuck, that's a lot of responsibility.
'Whoever I wanted to be.'

HER: Who do you want to be?

WOMAN: Who do I want to be?

I always knew what I was.
I was female. I was Black. Aged 9.
I was excited.
Delighted because I'd finally been invited to play with the
big kids!

I always knew what I was.
I was female. I was Black. Aged 17.
I was so sad, that I didn't leave my room for days,
I didn't know why though because
what have you got to be sad about when you're 17?

I always knew what I was.

I was female. I was Black. Aged 23. In New York City.

And I was happy. And I was happy. And I was happy –

– Why can't you just be happy?

There are people who have it worse than you!

Life's too short for you to be sad!

Have you tried meditating?

Have you tried yoga?

Have you tried taking vitamin D?

Cheer up love!

What doesn't kill you makes you stronger!

Everybody gets sad sometimes, you just have to learn not to wallow in it!

Why do you look so moody all the time?

You're in the prime of your life. You think you're stressed now? You don't know stress! Just wait until you're 30!

Just don't think about it.

… Depression? That's a very white, middle-class problem! You'd feel better if you went to church.

You'd feel better if you prayed.

You'd feel better if you spoke to God.

If you don't like feeling like this way, just stop.

You're kind of bringing down the mood here.

What have you got to be sad about?

Why don't you just go for a walk? That'll perk you up.

Why can't I just be happy?
A lot of people have it worse off than me.
What have I got to be sad about?
I'm in the prime of my life.
What doesn't kill me makes me stronger.

Why can't I just be happy?
A lot of people have it worse off than me.
What have I got to be sad about?
I'm in the prime of my life.
What doesn't kill me makes me stronger.

Why can't I just be happy?
A lot of people have it worse off than me.
What have I got to be sad about?
I'm in the prime of my life.
What doesn't kill me.

OFF THE EDGE

This is similar to Prologue but not the same.

So there's a girl. She's standing on a cliff. She looks out.
In the distance she sees a sea of tall, green trees. She sees
still, serene mountains. She sees a vast, blue sky.

She feels the breeze on her face and, as she walks towards
the edge of the cliff, she inhales deeply.

As she steps forward, she feels the ground shift. She looks
back and sees a crack has formed.

A small but sinister crack has formed.

She knows what comes next. She has to make a choice.
She has to make a decision.

She has to decide whether to go back, leap over the
crack, return to land that seems so stable, or throw herself
forward, off the edge, and hope she lands on something
soft, or stay exactly where she is, unmoving, and hope that
the ground doesn't fall from under her.

What does she do? What can she do?

There's one option.

But will she? Won't she? Will she? Won't she? Jump.

Off the edge. Jump. Do it. It's the only answer. It's the
only thing that makes sense. It's the only thing that makes
sense. It's the only thing that makes sense.

WAR WITH YOURSELF
(INTERLUDE)

Looping: She hits the mic to her chest to create a steady drum beat.

OHH OHH OHH OHH
(Repeat.)

YOU DON'T KNOW WHO YOU ARE.
YOU ARE BEING TORN APART FROM THE
INSIDE OUT.

YOU, YOU, YOU
(Repeat.)

ARE BEING TORN APART
(Repeat.)

YOU
(Repeat.)

DON'T KNOW, DON'T KNOW WHO YOU ARE
(Repeat.)

DOCTOR, DOCTOR

Looping: monotonous, repetitive, waiting room-style theme.

Tongue click.

> SITTING IN THE WAITING ROOM, I FEEL
> NERVOUS.
> I DON'T KNOW WHAT I PLAN TO SAY.
> SAY HE LOOKS AT ME
> AND SAYS THAT IT CAN'T BE
> 'CAUSE I'M TOO YOUNG TO NOT FEEL GREAT.
> PLUS I'VE GOT A ROOF OVER MY HEAD,
> A QUEEN-SIZE BED.
> WHAT REASON DO I HAVE TO FEEL THIS WAY?

WOMAN: So he calls me into his office…

Anyway… He calls me in and I sit down. I tell him that I've been feeling sad. But it feels like more than just sad.

It feels like I want to cry every second
                    of every hour
                              of every day.

It feels like I can't sleep.
          It feels like I can't breathe.
                    It feels like I can't eat.
I want to eat but I'm never hungry.

It feels like I want to disappear. It feels like I don't want to be here. It feels like I don't deserve to be here. It feels like I don't want to exist anymore.

I tell him that I've been feeling sad and I've tried everything.

I've looked online.

I've tried all of the self-help, self-care that you could try.

I've tried therapy and CBT.

I've tried meditation, drinking more water and breathing and doing yoga.

I've tried writing it down. I've tried writing it out.

I've tried talking it out and I can't take it anymore.

HE SAID 'KID YOU SOUND DEPRESSED.'
I SAID, DOCTOR, YES,
I'VE BEEN LIVING WITH THIS STRESS,
THIS PRESSURE ON MY CHEST.
I'VE TRIED EVERYTHING, EVERYTHING,
OVER AND OVER AND OVER.
BUT I JUST CAN'T GET OVER
HOW DOWN AND OUT I FEEL.

STARTED CRYING.
WELL NOT CRYING,
I AIN'T NO PUNK-ASS BITCH.
BUT SOMETIMES I FEEL EMOTIONS
JUST A LITTLE BIT.
SOMETIMES THEY OVERWHELM ME
AND I LOSE CONTROL.
SO RIGHT NOW IN THIS MOMENT I BARED
MY SOUL

I said, Doctor I know its name. I know what's wrong with me. And this can't be cured just with only therapy. I've tried everything I can try before coming and talking to you. Look I'm not against medication. I don't know what else to do.

HE SAID 'OKAY, I THINK YOU'RE RIGHT.
YOU HAVE TRIED EVERYTHING.
SO THIS IS WHAT I'LL DO
HERE'S WHAT I'M OFFERING.'

So he offers to put me on Citalopram.

HER looks confused and stops signing. WOMAN gestures to HER to interpret.

C-I-T-A-L-O-P-R-A-M.
10mg. A little pill that I'll take every day that will make me okay.
He says we'll see how you go, we'll give it a try. I take the green prescription paper and say 'Okay, thanks, bye.'
I go to the pharmacy, which is literally next door.
The woman hands me a box and says "Have you taken these before?"

I SAY NO,
SHE SAYS 'OKAY,
WELL, TAKE ONE A DAY.
THERE'S A LEAFLET IN THE BOX,
DON'T THROW IT AWAY.
IT HAS ALL THE INFORMATION THAT
YOU'RE GONNA NEED,
SO WHEN YOU GET A SECOND, GIVE IT
A READ.'

I leave the pharmacy. Get on the bus. And cry until I get home.

FLOATING

Looping: breathy vocals with a gentle rocking rhythm.

> I FEEL DROWSY,
> BUT APPARENTLY,
> THAT'S JUST A NORMAL WAY TO FEEL
> WHEN YOU FIRST TAKE THESE THINGS.

> AM I SUPPOSED TO FEEL THIS NUMB?
> I GUESS THAT'S BETTER
> THAN FEELING DAMAGED AND BROKEN
> FOREVER.

WOMAN sings a drowsy melody that drags through the music.

> OH
> OH

WOMAN records the melody into the loop station.

> OH
> OH

> OKAY, OKAY, I'LL TAKE THEM LIKE
> CLOCKWORK
> OKAY, OKAY, CAUSE THAT WILL MAKE MY
> BRAIN WORK.
> OKAY, OKAY, I'LL TAKE THEM EVERY DAY
> FOR THE REST OF MY LIFE, OKAY.

I FEEL DROWSY
BUT APPARENTLY...

Music begins to fade out.

WOMAN: *(To HER.)* Things like this shouldn't affect me cause
I'm a –

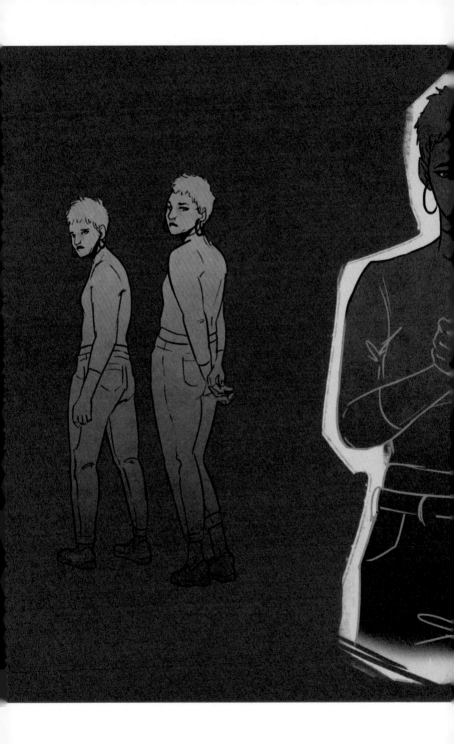

AN ODE TO THE STRONG, INDEPENDENT, BLACK WOMAN

WOMAN: Strong, independent, Black woman who don't need
no man.

Oh honey, don't he know I'm a strong, independent Black
woman who don't need no man.

I wish somebody would try me! Don't they know I'm a
strong, independent, Black woman who don't need no man!

So what have you got to be sad about? You're a –

Strong. Adjective. Definition:

Able to withstand force, pressure, or wear.

Having the power to move heavy weights or perform other
physically demanding tasks.

True. It's tasking to be a woman,

Little more to be a Black woman,

To always be that woman,

The strong woman,

Better-do-no-wrong woman,

Always being wronged,

Woman what have you got to be mad about?

I've got a lot to be mad about.

Solange told you so,

Though, I'll get over it again and again and again and again

And against all odds I'll pull through. Probably.

Just know there'll be more women being strong for you
Strong with you,
Strong Black woman without you who would the world
shit on?
So what have you got to be sad about when you're a strong...

Independent. Adjective. Definition:
Separate.
Not depending on another for livelihood or sustenance.

Starving to see yourself reflected on TV, in magazines, on
the big screen,
What do you mean you can't be seen?
No, Beyoncé doesn't count.
No, *Roots* doesn't count.
No, *12 Years A Slave* doesn't count.
No, the Black maid in the historical series doesn't count.
Because when you're only seen as the slave or the sassy
sista 'with an A'
Or the girl whose one line is 'heyyyy'
Or less than a line,
You get to say, the ever-glorious 'mmmhm'
So what have you got to be sad about when you're a
strong, independent...

Black. Adjective. Definition:
Of the very darkest colour owing to the absence of light.

Always aggressive in the absence of light
Perpetually tough in the absence of light
Sharp-tongued in the absence of light
GIFs of wagging fingers in the absence of light
Missing for 6 weeks in the absence of light
Missing for 6 months in the absence of light
Missing for 6 years in the absence of light

Sassy, Beastly, Angry

Unhuman, Unfeminine, Unprotected in the absence of light

Uniquely indestructible,

Only ever seen in the absence of light

So what have you got to be sad about when you're a
strong, independent...

Black. Adjective. Definition:

Of the very darkest colour owing to the absence of light or
the complete absorption of it.

WOMAN begins interpreting with HER.

So I must remind myself that I am light.

That I am love.

That I am whole.

I am enough.

I am weakness and strength.

I carry a weight on my back and balloons tied to my mind,

To remind myself to keep my head high.

I am not always strong but I have strength,

Although my fragility sings a high C in the ears of anyone
that will listen.

And so I'll remind you –

Signals for HER to stop signing. WOMAN continues signing.

– you strong, independent, Black women, that you are light.

That you are love.

That you are whole.

You are enough.

SIDE EFFECTS

WOMAN begins playing music from the loop station. It's similar to the Floating Song but not the same. It is heavier and drags more.

SIDE EFFECTS
SIDE EFFECTS
SIDE EFFECTS

I FEEL DROWSY
BUT I CAN'T SLEEP.
MY BRAIN IS CLOUDY
AND NOW I CAN'T THINK.

HER starts to add effects to the music and to the mic that WOMAN is singing into. She takes no notice and continues to sing and sign.

OH, HAVE I TAKEN ONE TODAY?
I CAN'T REMEMBER.
OH, DID I TAKE ONE YESTERDAY?
THIS WON'T BE GOOD FOR ME.

NO, GET OUT OF MY BRAIN.
NO, I CAN'T DO THIS AGAIN.
NO, WE'RE NOT ONE AND THE SAME.
NO, I CAN'T HANDLE THIS –

OKAY, OKAY, I'LL TAKE THEM LIKE
CLOCKWORK.
OKAY, OKAY, CAUSE THAT WILL MAKE
THESE PILLS WORK.

OKAY, OKAY, I'LL TAKE THEM LIKE
CLOCKWORK.
OKAY, OKAY, OKAY, OKAY.

I FEEL DROWSY...

HER stops the music suddenly.

BROKEN CLUBHOUSE

HER begins to click in the original Clubhouse tempo. HER records it. HER begins to sign 'Ooh, ohh, ohh' (three times) and 'Ooh! Ooh! Ooh!' WOMAN hesitantly joins in with no enthusiasm. HER begins to sign 'Welcome to the Clubhouse'. WOMAN hesitantly starts singing parts of the lyrics but trails off.

> *– CLUBHOUSE,*
> *WELCOME TO THE –*
> *WELCOME TO THE CLUBHOUSE*
> *COME ON IN*

Seeing that it's not working HER stops trying to loop.

HER: Hey there! We're so glad you could all join us back at The Clubhouse, we've missed you!

WOMAN doesn't translate. HER nudges WOMAN to join in.

Hey there! We're so glad you could all join us back at The Clubhouse, we've missed you!
Today we're going to talk about Friendship. Can we spell Friendship? F-R-I-E-N-D-S-H-I-P. Great job!
Friendship comes in many shapes and sizes. Do you remember our friend Sadness? Well our friend Sadness was kind enough to introduce us to a new friend, Citalopram.

WOMAN: Huh?

HER: Can we spell Citalopram? C-I-T-A-L–

WOMAN: – No, wait. –

HER: –O-P-R-A-M. Great job!

> Citalopram is such a good friend. They make sure I drink lots of water because when I'm around them my mouth gets very dry.
> But that's probably because I'm sweating so much, even though I'm not a little bit hot!
> Citalopram also makes me breathe like this *(Mimics shortness of breath.)*
> which is funny because it happens all the time. Even if I haven't been running!

Throughout, WOMAN is getting more and more confused.

HER: Sometimes when I'm with them I get really, really tired, and so they play this game with me where they won't let me sleep. It's really fun!

> They also do this amazing thing where they make everything around you seem soft and fuzzy. Like you're living inside of a cloud. And when you're walking home everything is in soft focus and although you know you're walking it feels like you're a zombie.

WOMAN: – Wait –

HER: Sometimes they make me feel a bit sick but that's okay because they will never let me throw up. They just make sure it feels like I'm going to throw up. But that would never happen because it keeps your stomach empty by hiding your appetite. Isn't that nice of them?

WOMAN: – Wait, stop. *(She stops translating.)*

HER: Stop? Why? We're having fun. We're learning about our new friend. Aren't you happy about that?

WOMAN: Yeah? Well no…

HER: What's the problem? I'm talking about our new friend. A good friend.

WOMAN: Yes but you're telling them all of the bad –

HER: Isn't this what you wanted? Aren't you having fun?

WOMAN: No, I'm not having fun. This isn't right. Why are you doing this?

HER: Because we don't hang out anymore. We don't do things together. Now that you're all buddy buddy with Citalopram, it's like you're trying to remove me.

WOMAN: Remove you? No it's not that, it's just…

HER: Look at what we've been through, together.

WOMAN: Whave have we been through together?

HER: We've done so much!
Remember that time when we were in that park and everything felt so horrible and we were drinking, what was it? Lager? That cheap stuff from the off-licence. Tasted awful. But we just drank and drank and drank. And then we went to the supermarket and bought all those over-the-counter pills.

WOMAN: – Stop –

HER: And you'd think that we would have thrown up everywhere but we didn't! Our stomach is basically made of steel.

WOMAN: – Stop –

HER: All I'm saying is we are so strong. Haven't I shown you that? Look at how strong we can be.

WOMAN: How strong we can be?

HER: Everyday we keep fighting the good fight. I need you. You need me–

WOMAN: – I don't need you.

HER: What do you mean you don't need me? Without me, you're weak. Without me, you're not interesting. I make you interesting. I give you depth. I give you something to talk about. I give you something to make theatre about. I make you a good artist. Without me, you wouldn't have anything interesting to say. No one would be interested in you. No one would pay attention to you.

WOMAN: – Stop, please –

HER: No one would pretend they care about you. Without me, no one would care about you. No one cares about you.

WOMAN: No one cares about you.

HER: You're just in the way. You're just a burden.

WOMAN: You're just a burden.

HER: You're just too much. People only pretend that they want to spend time with you because you're sick. They don't actually care.

WOMAN: They don't actually care.

HER: No. They just don't want to be named in the note you leave.
No one likes you. Even you don't like you. Why would you? Look at you. You're disgusting.

HER: You're not talented. Everything you've gotten has just been luck. You're the token. You're the diversity card. You get chosen because you tick boxes. You know that. You have nothing to offer the world.

Don't fool yourself into thinking that you have anything to offer. You are not important.

WOMAN: You're not important.

They speak and sign at the same time.

HER: You don't make a difference in the world. In fact, the world would be no different without you in it. You know that. You are a tiny blip in the universe. You don't matter to anyone. You don't matter. You don't matter. You don't matter.

WOMAN: I don't make a difference in the world. In fact, the world would be no different without me in it. I know that. I am a tiny blip in the universe. I don't matter to anyone. I don't matter. I don't matter. I don't matter.

SPIRALLING

A pre-recorded, remixed version of 'Floating' looping starts playing.
WOMAN notices.

> HOW AM I SUPPOSED TO FEED A MIND,
> INSIDE A BODY, THAT'S TRYING TO KILL ME?

WOMAN: So there's a girl. She's standing on a cliff. She looks out.
In the distance she sees a sea of tall, green trees. She sees
still, serene mountains. She sees a vast, blue sky.
She feels the breeze on her face and, as she walks toward
the edge of the cliff, she inhales deeply.

> HOW AM I SUPPOSED TO LIVE A LIFE,
> INSIDE THIS BODY, INSIDE THIS BODY,
> WITH A MIND THAT'S TRYING TO KILL ME?

As she steps forward, she feels the ground shift. She looks
back and sees a crack has formed.
A small but sinister crack has formed.
She knows what comes next. She has to make a choice.
She has to make a decision.
She has to decide whether to go back, leap over the
crack, return to land that seems so stable, or throw herself
forward, off the edge, and hope she lands on something
soft, or stay exactly where she is, unmoving, and hope that
the ground doesn't fall from under her.

> HOW AM I SUPPOSED TO LIVE A LIFE,
> INSIDE THIS BODY, WITH A MIND THAT'S
> TRYING TO KILL ME?

RIGHT NOW. HERE IS THE SAFEST PLACE TO
BE. I'M ON THE EDGE.

IT'S SAFER TO STAY WHERE YOU ARE
BECAUSE IF YOU STAY WHERE YOU ARE
THEN NOTHING CAN HURT YOU.

WOMAN ad-libs until she begins to arrive at a place of acceptance.

GOOD DAYS

WOMAN speaks and then signs at the same time. HER is pretending not to notice.

WOMAN: I just want to have good days. Not amazing days.
Not fantastic days. Not mind-blowing days. Just good days.
I deserve to have good days. Just good days.

I just want to be level. I don't want the extreme highs and the debilitating lows. I don't want the internal blows.

I want to wake up and look forward to my day. I want to believe that things are gonna be okay. I want to believe that I'll make it to tomorrow.

I'm tired of having to rebuild every day from scratch.
I'm tired of feeling brand new every day. I'm tired of having to build myself from nothing again and again and again. It's tiring.
But if that's what I have to do, okay.
Okay, I will build a new me every day. I will start from nothing every day. I'll keep making the same mistakes, if it means that once in a while I'll have a good day.
A real 'good day'.

The end.

ABOUT THE AUTHOR

Raised in Kilburn, North-West London, **Koko Brown** is a spoken word artist, theatre-maker and producer, who uses her loop station as an additional limb. She takes pride in her roots and creates work about being 'the other', focusing on race, mental health, gender, and identity.

An Alumni Associate Artist at **Ovalhouse** and Alumni Resident Artist at the **Roundhouse**, Koko was named one of 'seven new playwrights to look out for in 2019' in the *Evening Standard* and 'Ones To Watch: Best New Playwrights' in *Country & Town House*.

Koko has performed with venues such as the **National Theatre**, the **Lyric Hammersmith**, and the **Traverse Theatre** (Edinburgh). Her work has been performed at the **Roundhouse**, **Soho Theatre** and **Glastonbury Festival**.

Her debut show, **WHITE**, is also published by **Oberon Books** and was featured in *The Guardian* as one of their 'best shows at the Edinburgh Fringe Festival 2018'.

heykoko.com   **@TheKokoBrown**

<u>*By the same author*</u>

WHITE
9781786823847

WWW.OBERONBOOKS.COM

Follow us on Twitter @oberonbooks
& Facebook @OberonBooksLondon